ABSTRACT EXPRESSIONS

VOLUME TWO

UNIQUE COLORING BOOKS
FOR ALL AGES

By
VALERIE DOWDY

Dedicated to Scruffy,
...a brother, best friend, and family member.
You are missed.

Scruffy 2003-2015

Abraham & Scruffy

A portion from all sales of this coloring book will go to support Cairn Terrier Rescue
Thank you for your support~

VAD

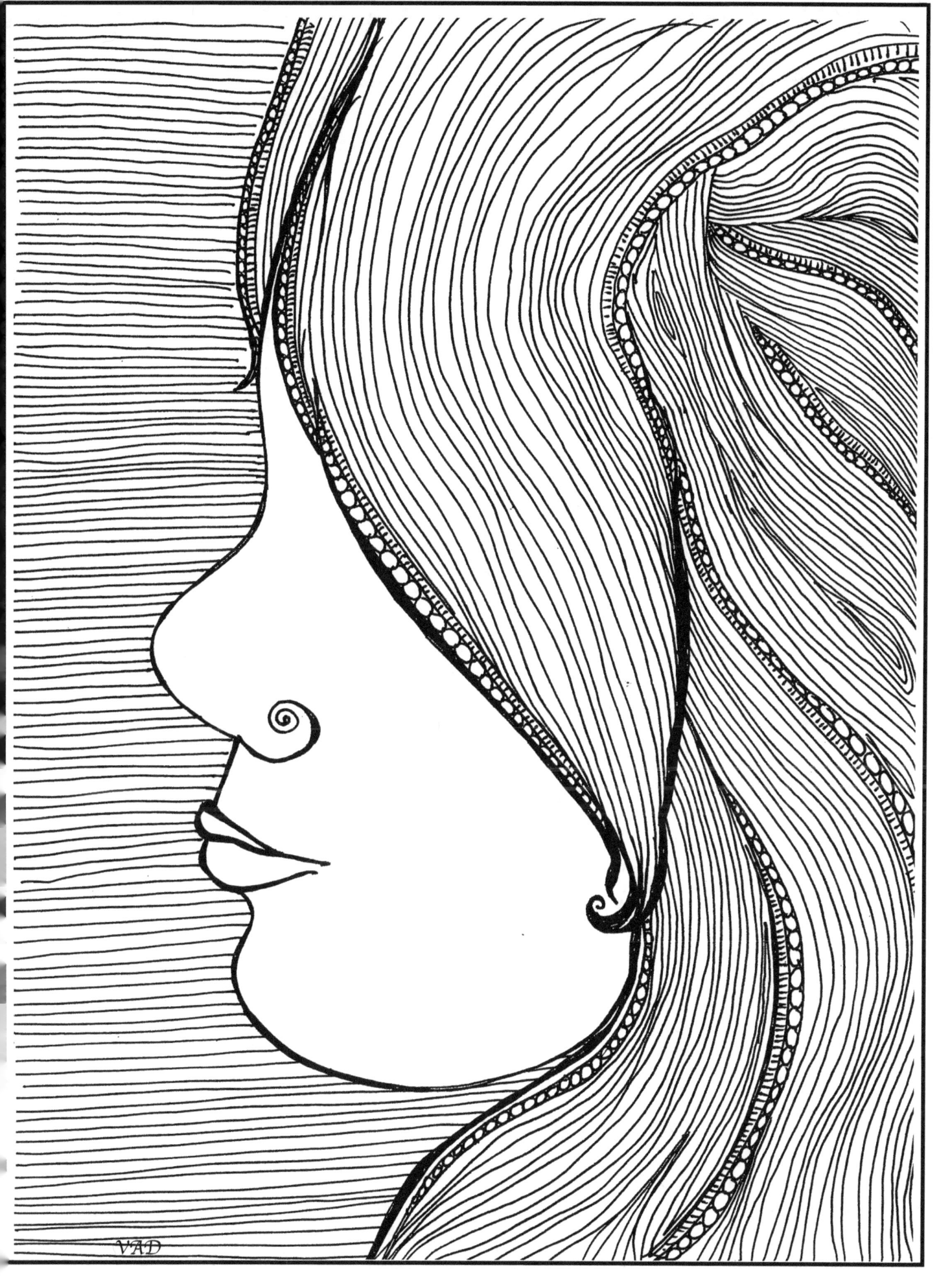

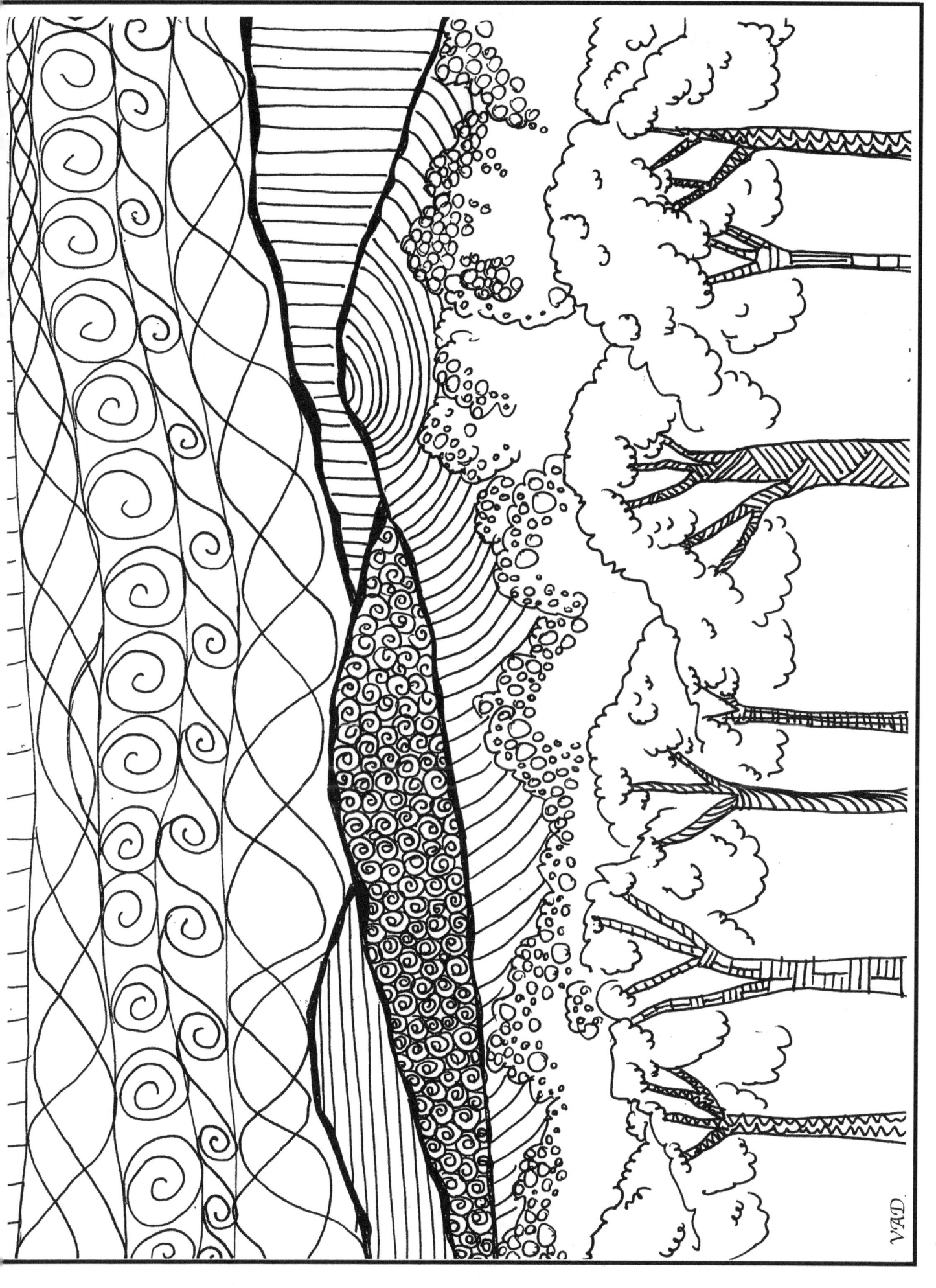

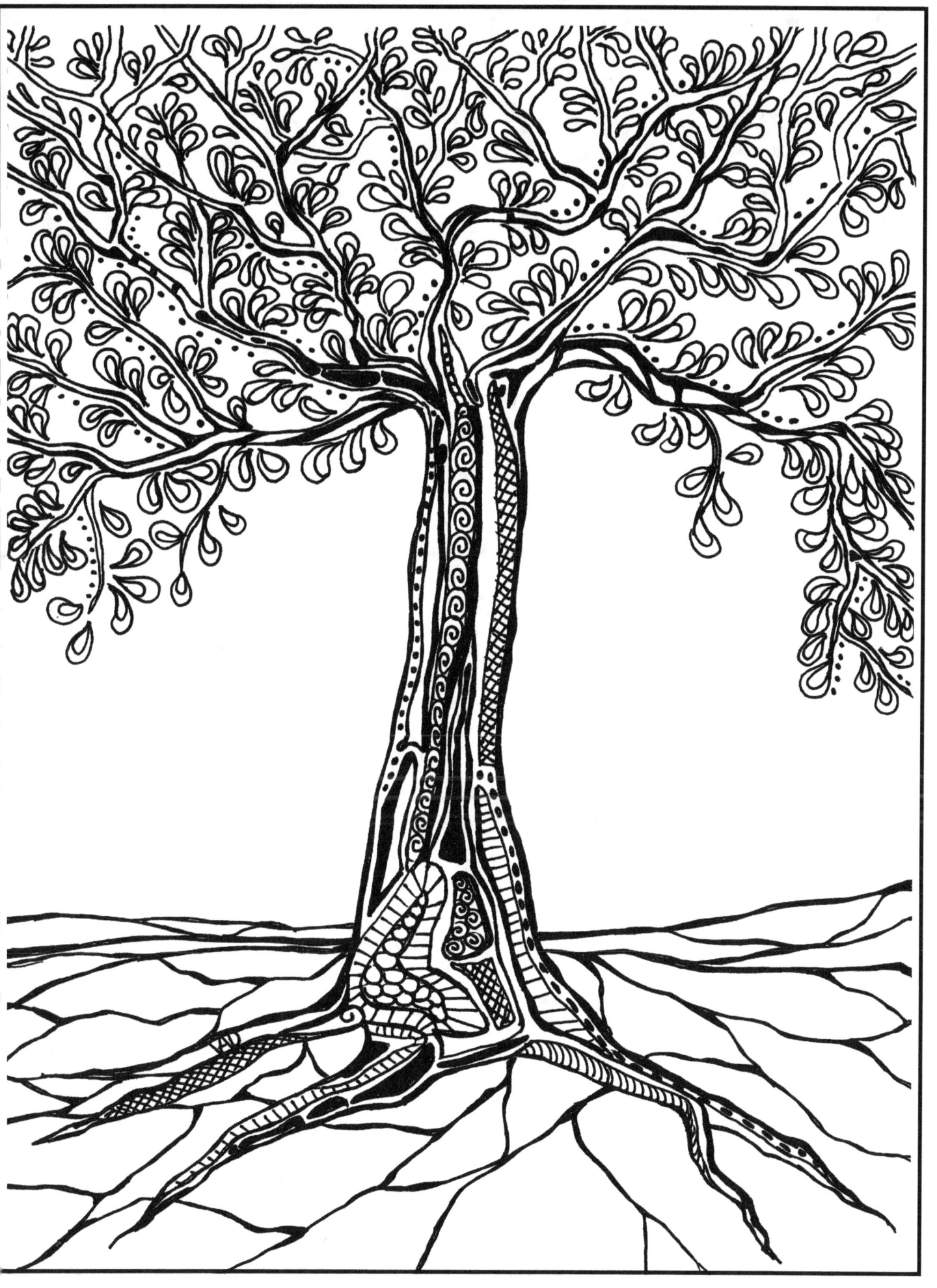

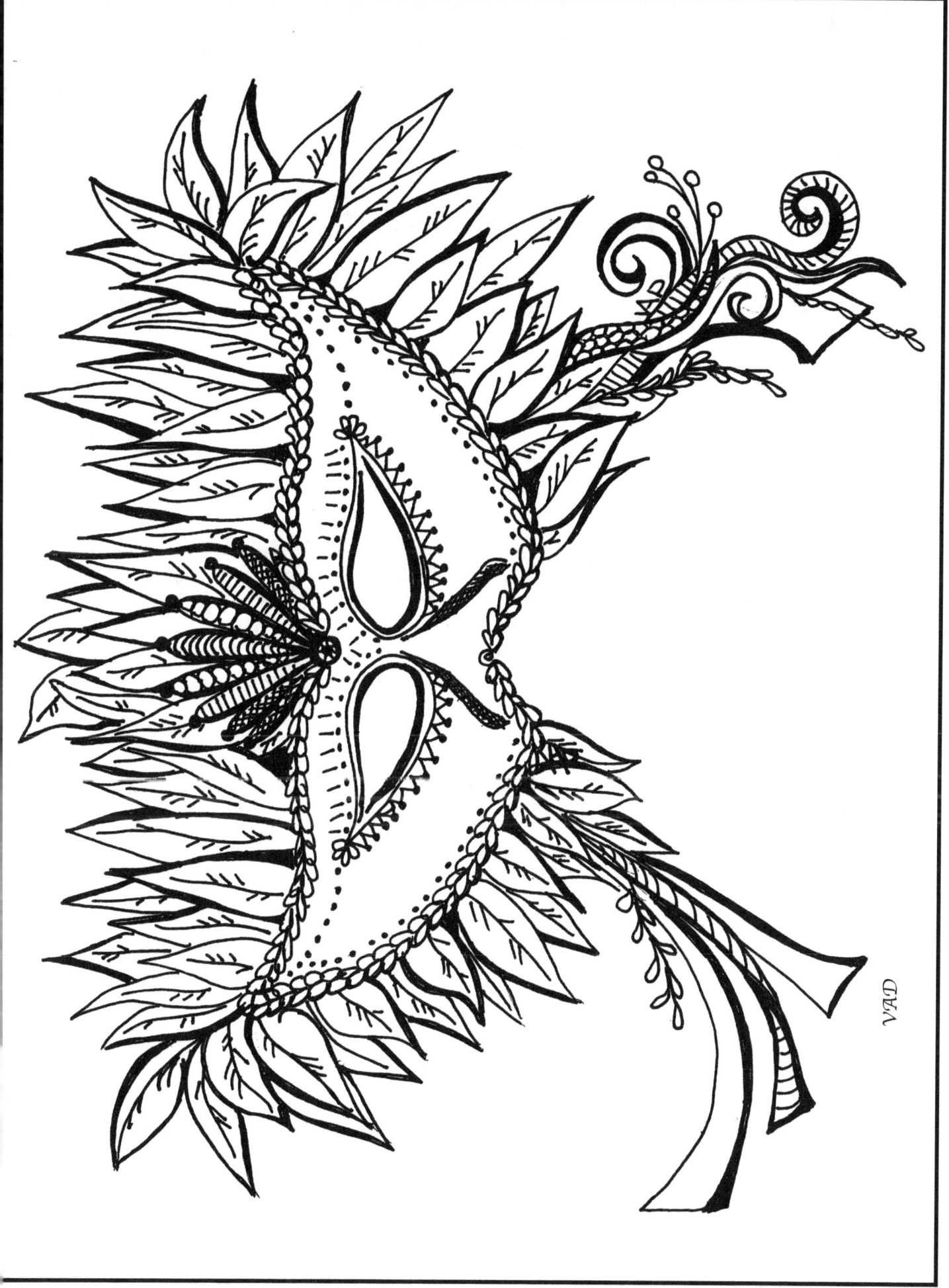

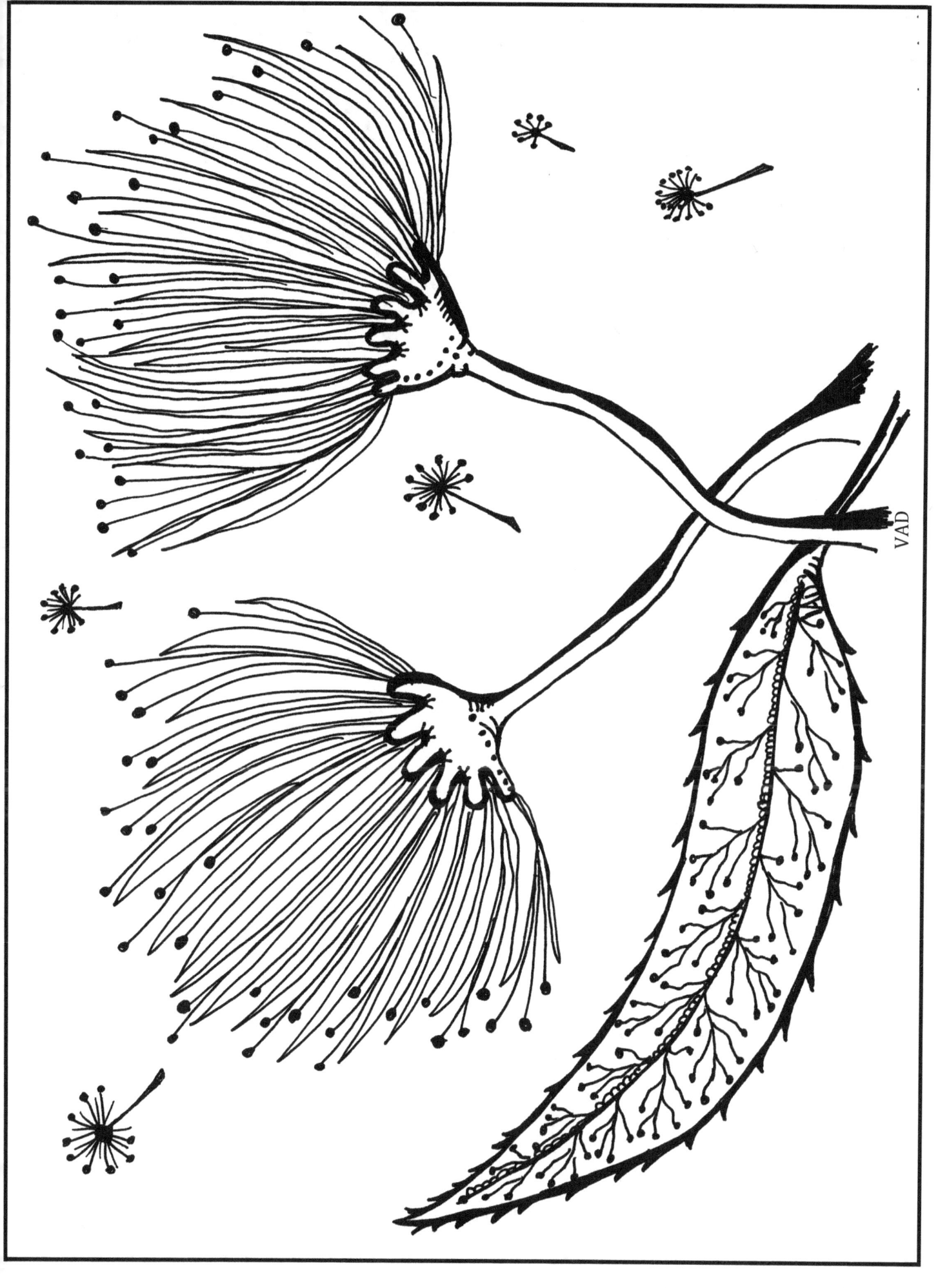

VAD

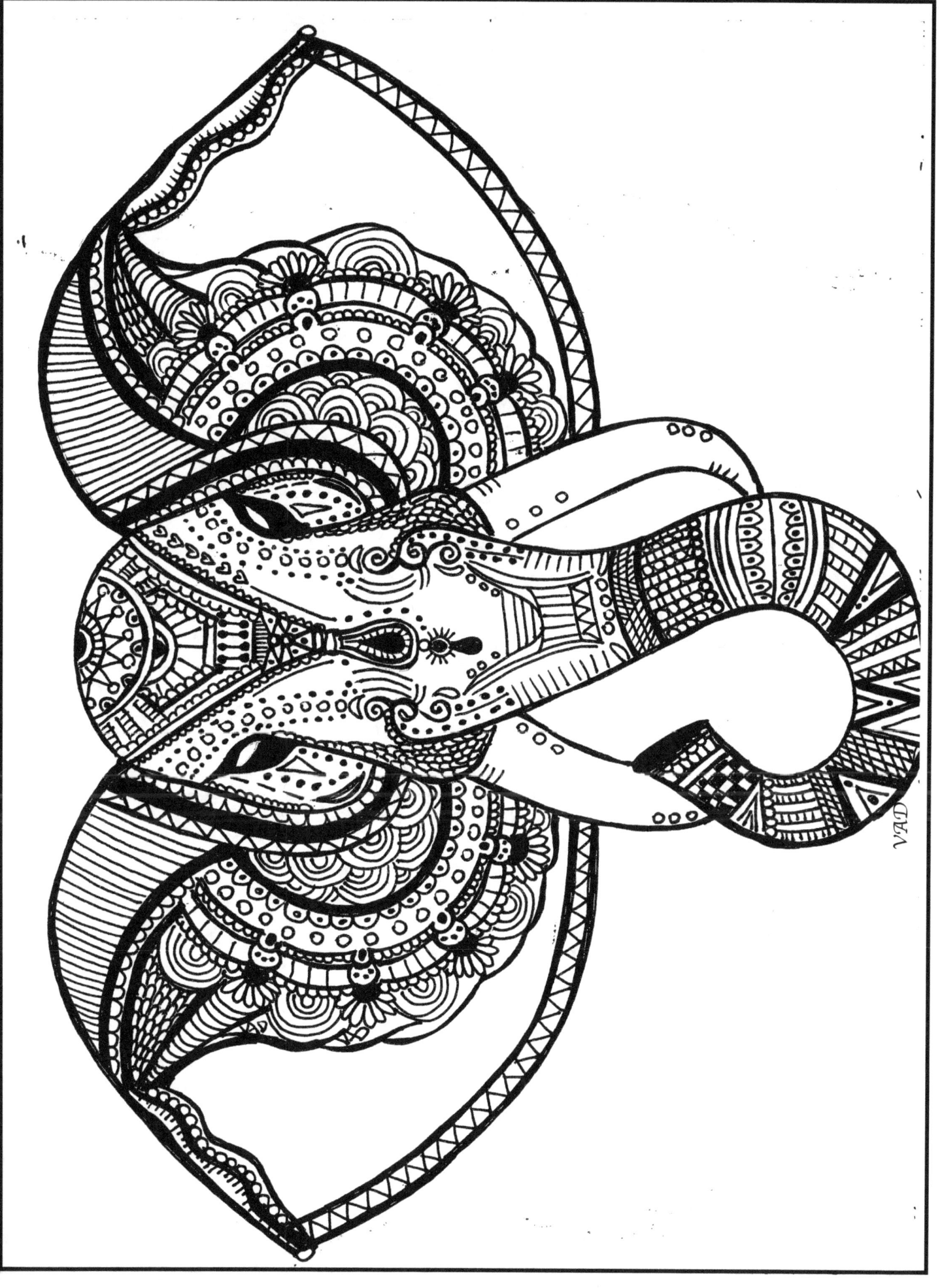

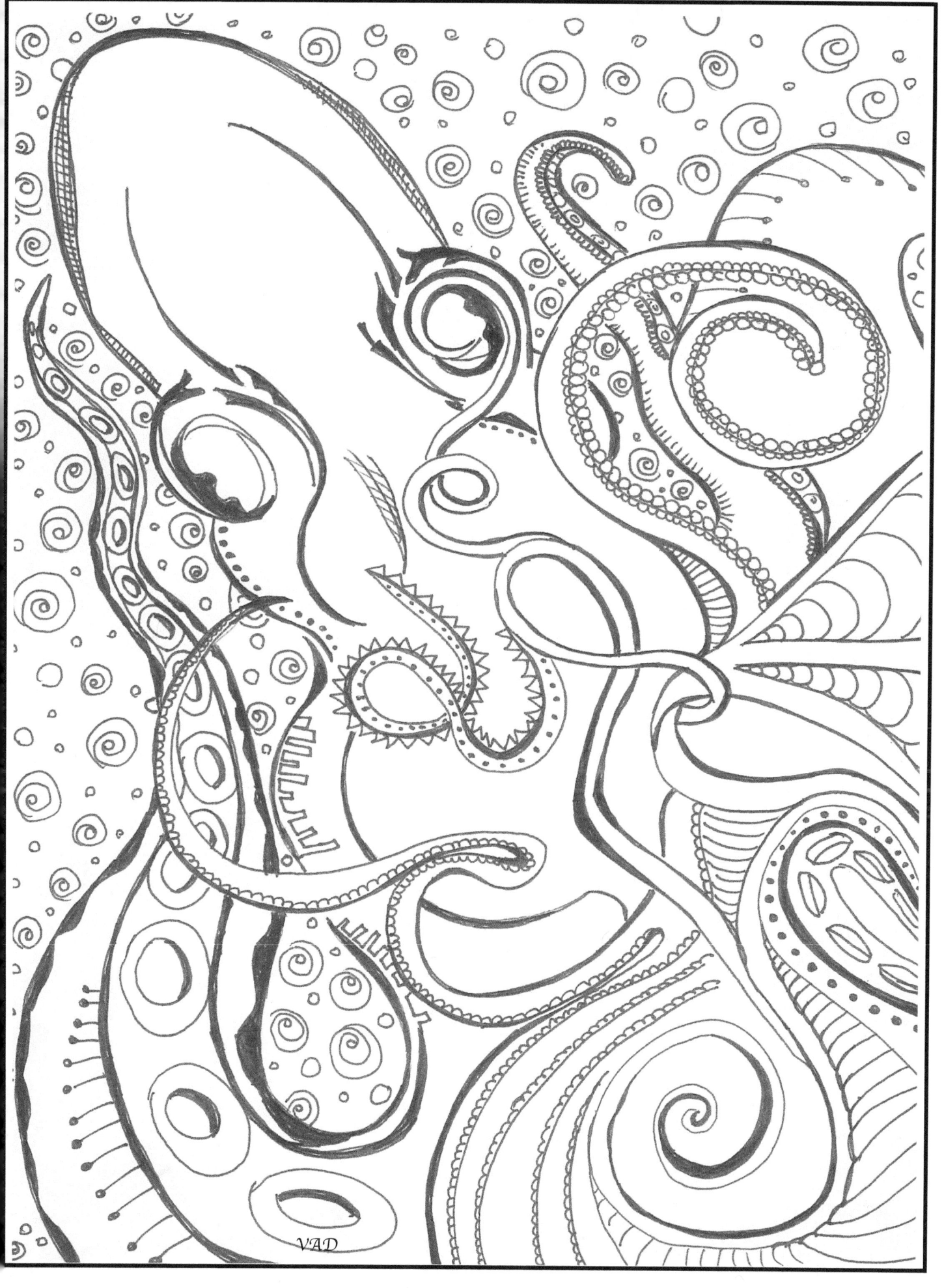

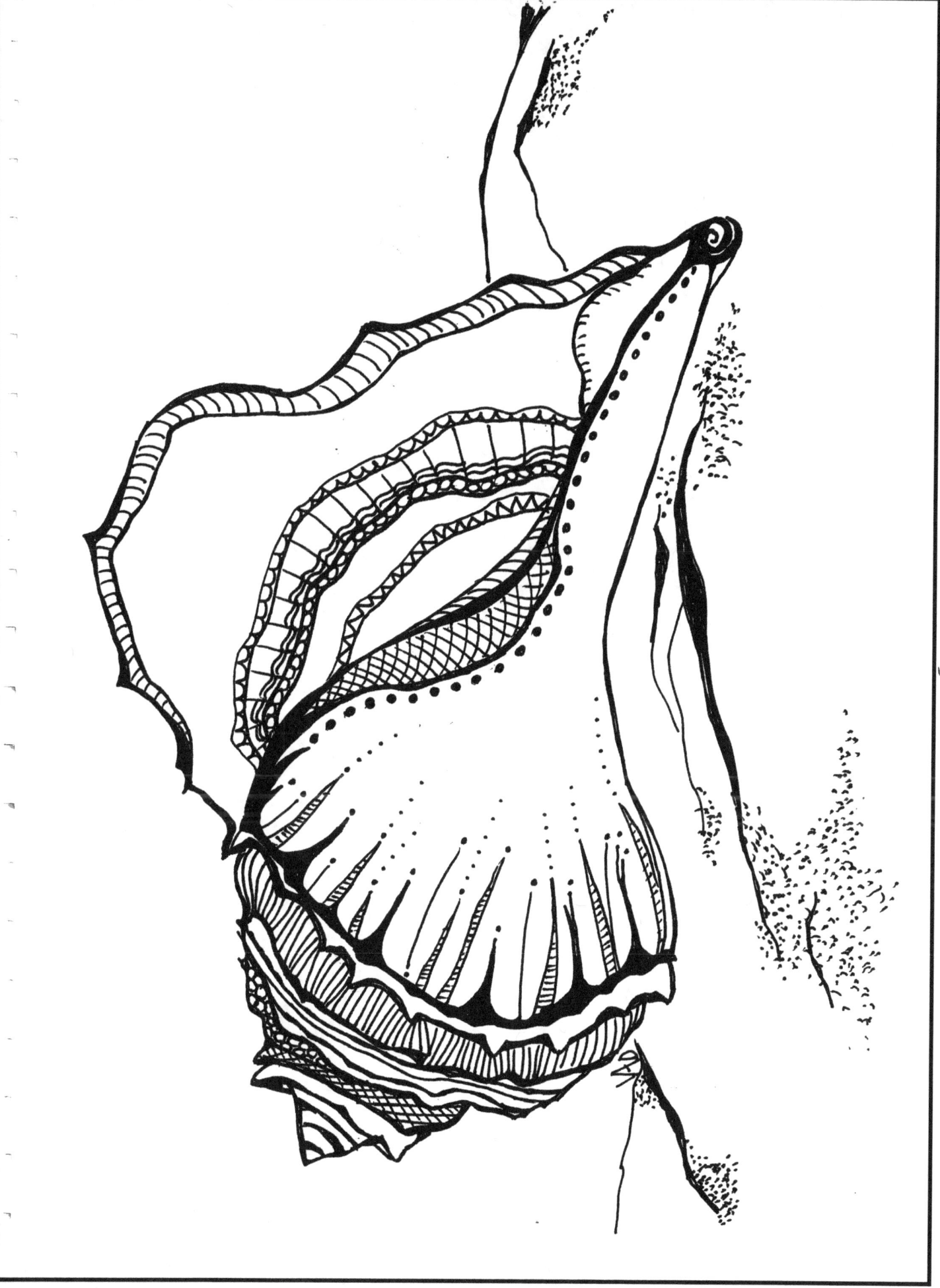

ABOUT THE AUTHOR

Valerie Dowdy is visual artist and recently coloring book creator. She lives in the mountains of Southwest Virginia, with her husband and one Cairn terrier, Abraham, where she also works part time as a paralegal. Valerie spends most of her free time either painting or hand drawing her images in to journals. She is developing a body of artwork that incorporates the intricate details of her drawings and fusing them together with the surrealism technique of her painting style. Using these journal entries she came up with her concept for "Abstract Expressions Volume One and Two". Literally tearing the illustrated pages from her books, Valerie composes coloring books in hopes of helping others focus, relax, and (re) connect with their own inner creativity.

www.ingramcontent.com/pod-product-compliance
Lightning Source LLC
Chambersburg PA
CBHW081133290526

45795CB00006B/2219